ISBN 978-1-331-51595-1
PIBN 10200550

For support please visit www.forgottenbooks.com

# Similar Books Are Available from
# www.forgottenbooks.com

**Poems**
by Edgar Allan Poe

**The Complete Poetical Works and Letters of John Keats**
by John Keats

**Erotica**
by Arthur Clark Kennedy

**The Complete Poetical Works of John Milton**
by John Milton

**One Hundred Poems of Kabir**
by Kabir

**The Barons' Wars, Nymphidia, and Other Poems**
by Michael Drayton

**A Book of English Poetry**
by George Beaumont

**Poems: Sonnets, Lyrics, and Miscellaneous**
by Edward Blackadder

**The Book of Fairy Poetry**
by Dora Owen

**Chinese Poems**
by Charles Budd

**Coleridge's The Rime of the Ancient Mariner**
And Other Poems, by Samuel Taylor Coleridge

**Complaints; Containing Sundrie Small Poemes of the Worlds Vanitie**
Whereof the Next Page Maketh Mention, by Edmund Spenser

**The Complete Poetical Works of Geoffrey Chaucer**
Now First Put Into Modern English, by John S. P. Tatlock

**Cursor Mundi (The Cursor of the World)**
A Northumbrian Poem of the XIVth Century, by Richard Morris

**The Defence of the Bride Other Poems**
by Anna Katharine Green

**The Divine Comedy, Vol. 1**
by Dante Alighieri

**The Duke of Gandia**
by Algernon Charles Swinburne

**Eanthe**
A Tale of the Druids, and Other Poems, by Sandford Earle

**The Earthly Paradise**
A Poem, by William Morris

**The English Poems of George Herbert**
Newly Arranged in Relation to His Life, by George Herbert Palmer

# Ministers' Hand-Book:

## FOR

## CHRISTENINGS, WEDDINGS, AND FUNERALS.

*COMPILED AND ARRANGED BY*

## M. J. SAVAGE.

GEORGE H. ELLIS, 101 MILK STREET.

1880.

# PREFACE.

I BEGAN the preparation of this manual simply as a Burial Service, and for my own convenience. I had found no one that just suited me. It was a trouble to select and arrange specially for each separate occasion. I wanted more variety. I did not like to carry two or three books with me, each of them being, perhaps, too large for the pocket. The habit of reading some appropriate verses, as a part of the service, increased this inconvenience. The desire to use the fitting thoughts of extra-Biblical writers increased it still more.

Learning my plan, other ministers have expressed a desire for copies. This explains why it is published.

When publication was determined on, it was thought best to include the services for Christening and Marriage. A service-book for the pocket will be found convenient where children are to be baptized or wedding ceremonies are to be performed at the house.

By selection and combination, it is hoped that both variety and adaptation to all ordinary occasions will be easily attained.

BOSTON, March, 1880.

# Contents.

# CONTENTS.

BLANK LEAVES (for other selections).

# Baptism of Children.

AND Jesus took a child and set him in the midst; and when he had taken him in his arms, he said unto them, Whosoever shall receive one of such children, in my name, receiveth me; and whosoever shall receive me, receiveth not me, but Him that sent me.

And they brought young children to him, that he should touch them; and his disciples rebuked those that brought them; but when Jesus saw it, he was much displeased, and said unto them, Suffer the little children to come unto me, and forbid them not, for of such is the kingdom of God. Verily I say unto you, Whosoever shall not receive the kingdom of God as a little child, he shall not enter therein.

Whosoever, therefore, shall humble himself as a little child, the same is greatest in the kingdom of heaven.

Take heed that ye despise not one of these little ones; for I say unto you, that in heaven their angels do always behold the face of my Father which is in heaven.

In sympathy, as we believe, with the spirit of Jesus, we are about to dedicate this child to God, in baptism. This water is the emblem of that purity which God desires in the souls of his children,— that purity which was in Jesus, his well-beloved Son, through whom we are called to pureness and holiness of living.

Will ye do your best to instruct this child in all the truth of God? And will ye faithfully endeavor to rear *him* in the nurture and admonition of the Lord?

*Answer* — We will.

Name this child.

*And, repeating the name, the Minister shall baptize the child, saying:*

I baptize thee in the name of the Father, and of the Son, and of the Holy Spirit.

*Or,*

In the faith, fellowship, and hope of the gospel, I dedicate thee to God, our Father in heaven.

Let us pray:

Almighty and everlasting God, who hast promised unto us that thou wilt not only be our God, but the God and father of our children, admit this child, we beseech thee, into the bosom of thy Church, into the service of all truth, into the arms of thy mercy, and into the communion of saints. Grant to *him* a healthful body, a good understanding, sweet dispositions, and rich measures of thy

Holy Spirit, that being steadfast in faith, joyful in hope, and rooted in charity, *he* may safely pass through the temptations of this world, and have part with thy faithful children in the life to come.

Endue these thy servants, O God, with wisdom from above. Help them in thine own best way to consecrate to thy service this cherished gift of thy goodness. By thy Holy Spirit aid them, and all who are here present, so to live before thee in love and obedience, as finally to see thy face in joy and peace eternal. Amen.

*A hymn may here be sung.*

The peace of God, which passeth all understanding, keep our minds and hearts in the knowledge and love of God, and of his Son Jesus Christ; and the blessing of God, the Father Almighty, be amongst us, and remain with us always. Amen.

# Marriage Service, No. 1.

---

*EPISCOPAL SERVICE,*
*(With slight changes.)*

DEARLY BELOVED, we are gathered together here, in the sight of God, and in the face of this company, to join together this man and this woman in holy matrimony; which is commended of Saint Paul to be honorable among all men: and therefore is not by any to be entered into unadvisedly or lightly; but reverently, discreetly, advisedly, soberly, and in the fear of God. Into this holy estate these two persons present come now to be joined. If any man can show just cause why they may not lawfully be joined together, let him now speak, or else hereafter for ever hold his peace.

*And also speaking unto the persons who are to be married, he shall say:*

I require and charge you both, as ye will answer at the day when the secrets of all hearts shall be disclosed, that if either of you know any impediment, why ye may not be lawfully joined together in matrimony, ye do now confess it. For be ye well assured, that if any persons are joined together otherwise than as God's law doth allow, their marriage is not lawful.

*The minister, if he shall have reason to doubt of the lawfulness of the proposed marriage, may demand sufficient surety for his indemnification : but if no impediment shall be alleged, or suspected, the minister shall say to the man :*

M., wilt thou have this woman to thy wedded wife, to live together after God's ordinance in the holy estate of matrimony ? Wilt thou love her, comfort her, honor, and keep her in sickness and in health; and, forsaking all others, keep thee only unto her, so long as ye both shall live?

*The man shall answer :*

I will.

*Then shall the minister say unto the woman :*

N., wilt thou have this man to thy wedded husband, to live together after God's ordinance in the holy estate of matrimony ? Wilt thou cherish and care for him, love, honor, and keep him in sickness and in health; and, forsaking all others, keep thee only unto him, so long as ye both shall live?

*The woman shall answer :*

I will.

*Then shall the minister say :*

Who giveth this woman to be married to this man ?

*Then shall they give their troth to each other in this manner. The minister, receiving the woman at her father's or*

*friend's hands, shall cause the man with his right hand
to take the woman by her right hand, and to say after him
as followeth :*

I, M., take thee, N., to my wedded wife, to have
and to hold from this day forward, for better, for
worse, for richer, for poorer, in sickness and in
health, to love and to cherish, till death us do
part, according to God's holy ordinance; and
thereto I plight thee my troth.

*Then shall they loose their hands; and the woman, with her
right hand taking the man by his right hand, shall like-
wise say after the minister :*

I, N., take thee, M., to my wedded husband, to
have and to hold from this day forward, for better,
for worse, for richer, for poorer, in sickness and in
health, to love and to cherish, till death us do
part, according to God's holy ordinance; and
thereto I give thee my troth.

*Then shall they again loose their hands; and the man shall
give unto the woman a ring. And the minister taking
the ring shall deliver it unto the man, to put it upon the
fourth finger of the woman's left hand. And the man
holding the ring there, and taught by the minister, shall
say :*

With this ring I thee wed, and with all my
worldly goods I thee endow: In the name of
our Father in Heaven. Amen.

*Then the man, leaving the ring upon the fourth finger of the
woman's left hand, the minister shall say ·*

Let us pray:

Giver of all good and fountain of all joy, the

guide, support, and felicity of all who put their trust in thee: we beseech thee to bless these thy servants. Enable them faithfully to perform the covenant they have now made in thy presence. May their hearts be united in the closest bonds of love. May they be counsel and strength, and light and comfort, one to the other; sharers of each other's joys, consolers of each other's sorrows, and helpers to each other in all the changes and chances of the world. Hand in hand, and heart with heart, trusting in each other and in thee, may they tread together the path of life. Be thou, O Father, their guard and guide. And lead them through this transitory world to the life eternal. Amen.

The Lord mercifully with his favor look upon you, and fill you with all spiritual benediction and grace; that ye may so live together in this life that in the world to come ye may have life everlasting. Amen.

# Marriage Service, No. 2.

———

NOTE.— The following service may suit the wants of those who do not like the form of *giving away* the bride,— a relic of the barbaric time when woman was *owned* and could be given away; as, also, those who — as bride or groom — do not like to take so large a part in the words of the service. It can be used without a ring, by omitting that part of the form. In that case, of course, the closing words would be changed, and might read: " I then, by virtue of authority," etc.

Of course the prayers, in either service, can be extempore, if the minister prefers.

If desired, the opening questions to both the man and the woman can be asked as one question; thus omitting the first answers (I do), and only answering once (I will).

*The parties standing arm in arm, the Minister shall say:*

DEAR FRIENDS, we have gathered here this {morning afternoon evening} to unite this man and this woman in holy marriage. This is an institution ordained by God in the very laws of our being, for the happiness and welfare of mankind. To be true, this outward ceremony must be but a symbol of that which is inner and real,—a sacred union of hearts that the Church may bless and the State make legal, but that neither can create or annul. To be happy, there must be a consecration of each to other, and of both to the noblest ends of life.

Believing that in such a spirit as this and with such a purpose you have now come, you may join your right hands.

### To the Man.

You, ———, take this woman, ———, for better, for worse, for richer, for poorer, to have and to hold, from this day forth, as your lawful wedded wife ?

*Ans.*—I do.

You will love, honor, cherish, and protect her in sickness and in health, in prosperity and in adversity, and, leaving all other, you will cleave only unto her, so long as you both shall live ?

*Ans.*—I will.

### To the Woman.

You, ———, take this man, ———, for better, for worse, for richer, for poorer, to have and to hold, from this day forth, as your lawful wedded husband ?

*Ans.*—I do.

You will love, honor, cherish, and care for him, in sickness and in health, in prosperity and in adversity, and, leaving all other, you will cleave only unto him, so long as you both shall live ?

*Ans.*—I will.

### To the Man.

What pledge do you offer that you will fulfil these vows ?

*Ans.*—This ring.

*He hands it to the Minister.*

*To the Woman.*

Do you, on your part, accept this in token of the same?

*Ans.*—I do.

*To the Man.*

*Handing back the ring.*

You will then place it on the fourth finger of the left hand.

*After this is done and they have again joined their right hands,*

*To them both.*

Forasmuch, then, as you have now pledged your mutual vows, and have given and received a ring in token of the same, I — by virtue of authority vested in me by the State, and in the name of our Father in heaven — pronounce you husband and wife.

Let us pray:

Our Heavenly Father, who hast set the human race in families, binding us together by these sacred and tender ties, these, thy children, have now, with clasped hands and mutual pledges, taken upon themselves these life-long obligations. We trust that it is indeed true that these outward acts only symbolize a union of hearts already made sacred by the holy love with which thou hast bound them together. From out the innumerable multitudes of earth these two have come, looked in each other's faces, and are made one. Their converging pathways have united, and henceforth are to be the same.

If it be possible, may their pathway be ever easy and pleasant beneath their feet. May the skies be ever sunny over their heads. But, if sorrow must come,— as it comes to all,— let the pressure of trial only bind them closer together. Let the experiences through which they pass only make them more and more completely one. With clasped hands and united hearts, may they accept life's joys and bear its burdens. And, if their sun goes down and night darkens their sky, may it at least be bright with the stars of hope.

And when the day of life is over, and the evening shadows fall, like tired, but happy children, may they come home to thee, and find the door of the Father's house wide open to their returning feet.

### BENEDICTION.

And now the Lord bless thee and keep thee ; the Lord make his face to shine upon thee, and be gracious unto thee ; the Lord lift up the light of his countenance upon thee, and give thee peace. Amen.

# Marriage Service, No. 3.

---

*For those who desire a brief service.*

STANDING, as you now do, in the presence of God and these witnesses, you covenant each to take the other as your companion and bosom friend for life. And you solemnly promise that you will continue to love, honor, and cherish each other ; that you will perform, in conscientious fidelity, in sickness and in health, in prosperity and in adversity, all the duties resulting from the marriage relation, so long as you both shall live ?

*Ans. each.*— I do.

*The ring, as in preceding service if desired.*

*Closing words (as in preceding).*

PRAYER AND BENEDICTION.

# Burial of the Dead.

---

## Death.

MAN, that is born of a woman, is of few days and full of trouble. He cometh forth like a flower, and is cut down: he fleeth as a shadow, and continueth not. Behold, thou hast made my days as a hand-breadth, and mine age is as nothing before thee. My days are swifter than a weaver's shuttle. They are passed away as the swift ships. There is but a step between me and death. All flesh is as grass, and all the glory of man as the flower of grass. The grass withereth, and the flower thereof falleth away.

(Men) dwell in houses of clay, whose foundation is in the dust. We are strangers before thee, and sojourners, as were all our fathers. Our days on the earth are as a shadow, and there is none abiding. Ye know not what shall be on the morrow. For what is your life? It is even a vapor, that appeareth for a little time, and then vanisheth away. See, then, that ye walk circumspectly, not as fools, but as wise, redeeming the time.

Lord, thou hast been our dwelling-place in all generations. Before the mountains were brought forth, or ever thou hadst formed the earth and the world, even from everlasting to everlasting, thou art God. Thou turnest man to destruction; and sayest, Return, ye children of men. For a thousand years in thy sight are but as yesterday when it is past, and as a watch in the night. Thou carriest them away as with a flood; they are as a sleep: in the morning they are like grass which groweth up. In the morning it flourisheth, and groweth up; in the evening it is cut down, and withereth. For we are consumed by thine anger, and by thy wrath are we troubled. Thou hast set our iniquities before thee, our secret sins in the light of thy countenance. For all our days are passed away in thy wrath: we spend our years as a tale that is told. The days of our years are threescore years and ten; and if by reason of strength they be fourscore years, yet is their strength labor and sorrow; for it is soon cut off, and we fly away. Who knoweth the power of thine anger? even according to thy fear, so is thy wrath. So teach us to number our days, that we may apply our hearts unto wisdom. O satisfy us early with thy mercy; that we may rejoice and be glad all our days. Make us glad according to the days wherein thou hast afflicted us, and the years wherein we have seen evil. Let thy work appear unto thy servants, and thy glory unto their children. And let the beauty of the Lord our God be upon us: and establish thou the work of our hands upon us; yea, the work of our hands establish thou it.

There is nothing that nature has made necessary which is more easy than death. What a shame is it, then, to stand in fear of anything so long that is over so soon! It is not death itself that is dreadful, but the fear of it that goes before it.

Why was such a one taken away in the prime of his years? Life is to be measured by action, not by time. A man may die old at thirty, and young at fourscore. Nay, the one lives after death ; and the other perished before he died. The fear of death is a continual slavery, as the contempt of it is certain liberty.

*Seneca.*

---

### Death of a Child.

And Jacob rent his clothes, and put sackcloth upon his loins, and mourned for his son many days. And all his sons and all his daughters rose up to comfort him ; but he refused to be comforted; and he said, For I will go down into the grave unto my son mourning. Thus his father wept for him.

---

And when the child was grown, it fell on a day that he went out to his father to the reapers. And he said unto his father, My head, my head. And he said to a lad, Carry him to his mother. And when he had taken him, and brought him to his mother, he sat on her knees till noon, and then died. And she went up, and laid him on the bed of the man of God, and shut the door upon him, and went out. And she called unto her husband, and said, Send me, I pray thee, one of the young men, and one of the asses, that I may run to the man of God, and come again. And he said, Wherefore wilt thou go to him to-day? it is neither new moon, nor sabbath. And she said, It shall be well. Then she saddled an ass, and said to her servant, Drive, and go forward; slack not thy riding for me, except I bid thee. So she went and came unto the man of God to Mount Carmel. And it came to pass, when the man of God saw her afar off, that he said to Gehazi his servant, Behold, yonder is that Shunamite: run now, I pray thee, to meet her, and say unto her, Is it well with thee? is it well with thy husband? is it well with the child? And she answered, It is well.

---

David therefore besought God for the child; and David fasted, and went in, and lay all night upon the earth. And the elders of his house arose, and went to him, to raise him up from the earth; but he would not, neither did he eat bread with them. And it came to pass on the seventh day that the child died. And the servants of David feared to tell him that the child was dead: for they said, Behold, while the child was yet alive, we spake unto him, and he would not hearken unto our voice: how will he then vex himself, if we tell him that the child is dead? But when David saw that his servants whispered, David perceived that the child was dead: therefore David said unto his servants, Is the child dead? And they said, He is dead. Then David arose from the earth, and washed, and anointed himself, and changed his apparel, and came into the house of the Lord, and worshipped: then he came to his own house; and when he required, they set bread before him, and he did eat. Then said his servants unto him, What thing is this that thou hast done? thou didst fast and weep for the child, while it was alive; but when the child was dead, thou didst rise and eat bread. And he said, While the child was yet alive, I fasted and wept: for I said, Who can tell whether God will be gracious to me, that the child may live? But now he is . dead, wherefore should I fast? can I bring him back again? I shall go to him, but he shall not return to me.

---

And they brought young children to him, that he should touch them: and his disciples rebuked those that brought them. But when Jesus saw it, he was much displeased, and said unto them, Suffer the little children to come unto me, and forbid them not: for of such is the kingdom of God. Verily I say unto you, Whosoever shall not receive the kingdom of God as a little child, he shall not enter therein. And he took them up in his arms, put his hands upon them, and blessed them.

---

A Hindoo mother gave birth to a son. When the boy was able to walk by himself, he died. The young mother carried the dead child clasped to

her bosom, and went from house to house, asking
if any one could give her medicine for it. Some
regarded her as mad; but a wise man said · "I
cannot cure your son, but I know of one who can
attend to it. You must go to him: he can give
medicine."

Then she went to him, and said, "Lord and
master, do you know any medicine that will be
good for my boy?" He answered, "I know of
some." She asked, "What medicine do you re-
quire?" The sage replied, "I require a handful
of mustard-seed taken from a house where no
son, husband, parent, or servant has died." The
mother then went about with her dead child, ask-
ing for the mustard-seed. The people said, "Here
is some mustard-seed: take it" Then she asked,
"In my friend's house has there died a son, a
husband, a parent, or a servant?" They replied:
"What is this you say? The living are few, but
the dead are many."

Then she went to other houses; but one said,
"I have lost my son;" another, "I have lost my
parent;" until at last she said: "This is a heavy
task I have undertaken. I am not the only one
whose son is dead. In the whole country, children
are dying, parents are dying."

The woman went and laid her child down in the
forest, and then came to the teacher. He said to
her, "Have you received the handful of mustard-
seed?" She answered: "I have not: the people
of the village told me, The living are few, but the
dead are many." Then he said to her, "You
thought that you alone had lost a son: the law of
death rules all."

Then the mother devoted herself to helping others.

*With slight changes, from Conway's version of one of Buddha's Parables.*

---

### The Sorrow of Bereavement.

Then Job arose, and rent his mantle, and shaved his head, and fell down upon the ground, and worshipped. And said, Naked came I out of my mother's womb, and naked shall I return: the Lord gave, and the Lord hath taken away; blessed be the name of the Lord.

After this opened Job his mouth, and cursed his day. And Job spake, and said, Let the day perish wherein I was born. Let that day be darkness; let not God regard it from above, neither let the light shine upon it. Let darkness and the shadow of death stain it; let a cloud dwell upon it; let the blackness of the day terrify it. As for that night, let darkness seize upon it; let it not be joined unto the days of the year, let it not come into the number of the months. Lo, let that night be solitary, let no joyful voice come therein. Let the stars of the twilight thereof be dark; let it look for light, but have none; neither let it see the dawning of the day.

For now should I have lain still and been quiet, I should have slept: then had I been at rest. There the wicked cease from troubling; and there the weary be at rest. There the prisoners rest together; they hear not the voice of the oppressor.

The small and great are there ; and the servant is free from his master. ·Wherefore is light given to him that is in misery, and life unto the bitter in soul ; which long for death, but it cometh not ; and dig for it more than for hid treasures ; which rejoice exceedingly, and are glad when they can find the grave? Why is light given to a man whose way is hid, and whom God hath hedged in ?

As the hart panteth after the water-brooks, so panteth my soul after thee, O God. My soul thirsteth for God, for the living God : when shall I come and appear before God ? My tears have been my meat day and night, while they continually say unto me, Where is thy God? When I remember these things, I pour out my soul in me ; for I had gone with the multitude, I went with them to the house of God, with the voice of joy and praise, with a multitude that kept holyday. Why art thou cast down, O my soul? and why art thou disquieted in me? hope thou in God ; for I shall yet praise him for the help of his countenance. O my God, my soul is cast down within me : therefore will I remember thee. Deep calleth unto deep at the noise of thy waterspouts : all thy waves and thy billows are gone over me. Yet the Lord will command his loving-kindness in the daytime, and in the night his song shall be with me, and my prayer unto the God of my life. I will say unto God my rock, Why hast thou forgotten me? why go I mourning because of the oppression of the enemy ? As with a sword in my bones, mine enemies reproach me ; while they say daily unto me, Where is thy God? Why art thou cast down, O my soul? and why art thou disquieted within me? hope thou in God: for I shall yet praise him, who is the health of my countenance, and my God.

———

Next to the encounter of death in our own bodies, the most sensible calamity is the death of a friend. It were inhumanity, and not virtue, not to be moved. In such cases, we cannot command ourselves: we cannot forbear weeping, and we ought not to forbear. We may accuse fate, but we cannot alter it: it is not to be removed either with reproaches or tears. They may carry us to the dead, but never bring them back again to us. To mourn without measure is folly; and not to mourn at all is insensibility.

The comfort of having a friend may be taken away, but not that of having had one. In some respects, I have lost what I have had; in others, I still retain what I have lost. It is an ill construction of Providence to reflect only upon my friend's being taken away, without any regard to the benefit of his being once given me.

Let us therefore make the best of our friends while we have them. He that has lost a friend has more cause of joy that he once had him, than of grief that he is taken away. That which is past we are sure of. It is impossible to make it not to have been. But there is no applying of consolation to fresh and bleeding sorrow: the very discourse irritates the grief and inflames it.

*Seneca.*

## The Discipline of Sorrow.

Blessed be God, even the Father of our Lord
Jesus Christ, the Father of mercies, and the God
of all comfort; who comforteth us in all our trib-
ulation, that we may be able to comfort them which
are in any trouble, by the comfort wherewith we
ourselves are comforted of God. Wait on the
Lord; be of good courage, and he shall strengthen
thy heart; wait, I say, on the Lord. Weeping
may endure for a night, but joy cometh in the
morning. He doth not afflict willingly, nor grieve
the children of men. And ye have forgotten the
exhortation which speaketh unto you as unto chil-
dren, My son, despise not thou the chastening of
the Lord, nor faint when thou art rebuked of him:
for whom the Lord loveth he chasteneth, and
scourgeth every son whom he receiveth. If ye
endure chastening, God dealeth with you as with
sons; for what son is he whom the father chasten-
eth not? Furthermore we have had fathers of
our flesh which corrected us, and we gave them
reverence: shall we not much rather be in sub-
jection unto the Father of spirits, and live? For
they verily for a few days chastened us after their
own pleasure; but he for our profit, that we might
be partakers of his holiness. Now no chastening
for the present seemeth to be joyous, but griev-
ous: nevertheless afterward it yieldeth the peace-
able fruit of righteousness unto them which are
exercised thereby. Wherefore lift up the hands
which hang down, and the feeble knees; and
make straight paths for your feet, lest that which

is lame be turned out of the way; but let it rather be healed.

For which cause we faint not; but though our outward man perish, yet the inward man is renewed day by day. For our light affliction, which is but for a moment, worketh for us a far more exceeding and eternal weight of glory; while we look not at the things which are seen, but at the things which are not seen: for the things which are seen are temporal; but the things which are not seen are eternal. Affliction cometh not forth of the dust, neither doth trouble spring out of the ground. Happy is the man whom God correcteth. Therefore despise not the chastening of the Almighty. For he maketh sore, and bindeth up; he woundeth, and his hands make whole.

The Lord is my shepherd; I shall not want. He maketh me to lie down in green pastures: he leadeth me beside the still waters. He restoreth my soul: he leadeth me in the paths of righteousness for his name's sake. Yea, though I walk through the valley of the shadow of death, I will fear no evil: for thou art with me; thy rod and thy staff they comfort me. Thou preparest a table before me in the presence of mine enemies: thou anointest my head with oil; my cup runneth over. Surely goodness and mercy shall follow me all the days of my life; and I will dwell in the house of the Lord forever.

The Lord is my light and my salvation; whom shall I fear? the Lord is the strength of my life; of whom shall I be afraid? Though an host should encamp against me, my heart shall not fear: though war should rise against me, in this will I be confident. One thing have I desired of the Lord, that will I seek after; that I may dwell in the house of the Lord all the days of my life, to behold the beauty of the Lord, and to inquire in his temple. For in the time of trouble he shall hide me in his pavilion: in the secret of his tabernacle shall he hide me; he shall set me up upon a rock. And now shall mine head be lifted up above mine enemies round about me: therefore will I offer in his tabernacle sacrifices of joy; I will sing, yea, I will sing praises unto the Lord. Hear, O Lord, when I cry with my voice: have mercy also upon me, and answer me. When thou saidst, Seek ye my face; my heart said unto thee, Thy face, Lord, will I seek. Hide not thy face far from me; put not thy servant away in anger: thou hast been my help; leave me not, neither forsake me, O God of my salvation. When my father and my mother forsake me, then the Lord will take me up. Teach me thy way, O Lord, and lead me in a plain path. I had fainted, unless I had believed to see the goodness of the Lord in the land of the living. Wait on the Lord: be of good courage, and he shall strengthen thine heart: wait, I say, on the Lord.

He that dwelleth in the secret place of the Most High shall abide under the shadow of the Almighty. I will say of the Lord, He is my refuge, and my fortress: my God; in him will I trust. Surely he shall deliver thee from the snare of the fowler, and from the noisome pestilence. He shall cover thee with his feathers, and under his wings shalt thou trust: his truth shall be thy shield and buckler. Thou shalt not be afraid for the terror by night, nor for the arrow that flieth by day. Nor for the pestilence that walketh in darkness, nor for the destruction that wasteth at noonday. Because thou hast made the Lord, which is my refuge, even the Most High, thy habitaiton, there shall no evil befall thee, neither shall any plague come nigh thy dwelling For he shall give his angels charge over thee, to keep thee in all thy ways. They shall bear thee up in their hands, lest thou dash thy foot against a stone. Because he hath set his love upon me, therefore will I deliver him: I will set him on high, because he hath known my name. He shall call upon me, and I will answer him: I will be with him in trouble; I will deliver him, and honor him. With long life will I satisfy him, and shew him my salvation.

---

## The Hope of Immortality.

For there is hope of a tree, if it be cut down, that it will sprout again, and that the tender branch thereof will not cease. Though the root thereof wax old in the earth, and the stock thereof die in the ground; yet through the scent of water it will bud, and bring forth boughs like a plant. But man dieth, and wasteth away: yea, man giveth up the ghost, and where is he? As the waters fail from the sea, and the flood decayeth and drieth up: so man lieth down, and riseth not: till the heavens be no more, they shall not awake, nor be raised out of their sleep. O that thou wouldst hide me in the grave, that thou wouldst keep me secret, until thy wrath be past, that thou wouldst appoint me a set time, and remember me! If a man die, shall he live again? all the days of my appointed time will I wait, till my change come. Thou shalt call, and I will answer thee: thou wilt have a desire to the work of thine hands. My heart and my flesh faileth, but God is the strength of my heart and my portion forever.

The last enemy that shall be destroyed is death. But some man will say, How are the dead raised up? and with what body do they come? That which thou sowest is not quickened, except it die: and that which thou sowest, thou sowest not that body that shall be, but God giveth it a body as it hath pleased him, and to every seed his own body. All flesh is not the same flesh: but there is one kind of flesh of men, another flesh of beasts, another of fishes, and another of birds. There are also celestial bodies and bodies ter- restrial; but the glory of the celestial is one, and the glory of the terrestrial is another. There is one glory of the sun, and another glory of the moon, and another glory of the stars; for one star differeth from another star in glory. So also is the higher life of the dead. It is sown in cor- ruption; it is raised in incorruption: it is sown in dishonor; it is raised in glory: it is sown in weakness; it is raised in power: it is sown a natural body; it is raised a spiritual body. There is a natural body, and there is a spiritual body.

Howbeit that was not first which is spiritual, but that which is natural ; and afterward that which is spiritual. As is the earthy, such are they also that are earthy ; and as is the heavenly, such are they also that are heavenly. And as we have borne the image of the earthy, we shall also bear the image of the heavenly. Now this I say, brethren, that flesh and blood cannot inherit the kingdom of God ; neither doth corruption inherit incorruption. For this corruptible must put on incorruption, and this mortal must put on immortality. So when this corruptible shall have put on incorruption, and this mortal shall have put on immortality, then shall be brought to pass the saying that is written, Death is swallowed up in victory. O death, where is thy sting ? O grave, where is thy victory ?

For we know that if our earthly house of this tabernacle were dissolved, we have a building of God, an house not made with hands, eternal in the heavens. For in this we groan, earnestly desiring to be clothed upon with our house which is from heaven : if so be that being clothed we shall not be found naked. For we that are in this tabernacle do groan, being burdened : not for that we would be unclothed, but clothed upon, that mortality might be swallowed up of life. And the ransomed of the Lord shall return, and come to Zion with songs and everlasting joy upon their heads : they shall obtain joy and gladness, and sorrow and sighing shall flee away. And I heard a voice from heaven saying, Write, Blessed are the dead which die in the Lord from henceforth. Yea, saith the Spirit, that they may rest from their labors ; and their works do follow them. They shall hunger no more, neither thirst any more ; neither shall the sun light on them, nor any heat. And God shall wipe away all tears from their eyes.

And the city had no need of the sun, neither of the moon to shine in it ; for the glory of God did lighten it. And the nations of them which are saved shall walk in the light of it; and the kings of the earth do bring their glory and honor into it. And the gates of it shall not be shut at all by day ; and there shall be no night there.

And I heard a great voice out of heaven saying, Behold, the tabernacle of God is with men, and he will dwell with them, and they shall be his people, and God himself shall be with them, and be their God. And God shall wipe away all tears from their eyes ; and there shall be no more death, neither sorrow, nor crying, neither shall there be any more pain : for the former things are passed away.

——————

This life is only a prelude to eternity, where we are to expect another state of things. We have no prospect of heaven here, but at a distance : let us, therefore, expect our last hour with courage. The last I say to our bodies, but not to our minds. The day which we fear as our last is but the birth-day of eternity. What we fear as a rock proves to be a harbor. He who dies young has only made a quick voyage of it. What if death comes? If it does not stay with us, why should we fear it?

What it is we know not. And it were rash to condemn what we do not understand. But this we presume, either we shall pass out of this life into a better one, where we shall live in diviner mansions, or else return to our first principles, free from any sense of inconvenience.

That which we call death is but a pause or suspension, and in truth a progress to life : only our thoughts look downward upon the body, and not forward upon things to come. It is the care of a wise and good man to look to his manners and actions ; and rather how well he lives than how long. To die sooner or later is not the business, but to die well or ill; for death brings us to immortality.

*Seneca.*

————

Oh may I join the choir invisible
Of those immortal dead who live again
In minds made better by their presence : live
In pulses stirred to generosity,
In deeds of daring rectitude, in scorn
For miserable aims that end with self,
In thoughts sublime that pierce the night like stars,
And with their mild persistence urge man's search
To vaster issues.— So to live is heaven :
To make undying music in the world,
Breathing as beauteous order, that controls
With growing sway the growing life of man.
         .... This is life to come,
Which martyred men have made more glorious
For us who strive to follow. May I reach
That purest heaven ; be to other souls
The cup of strength in some great agony;
Enkindle generous ardor; feed pure love;
Beget the smiles that have no cruelty ;
Be the sweet presence of a good diffused,

And in diffusion ever more intense.
So shall I join the choir invisible,
Whose music is the gladness of the world.

*George Eliot.*

————

The soul lives after the body dies. The soul passes through the gate; he makes a way in the darkness to his Father. He has pierced the heart of evil, to do the things of his Father. He has come a prepared Spirit. He says: Hail, thou Self-Created! Do not turn me away. I am one of thy types on earth. I have not privily done evil against any man; I have not been idle; I have not made any to weep; I have not murdered; I have not defrauded; I have not committed adultery. I am pure.

*The Judge of the Dead answers:*

Let the soul pass on. He is without sin; he lives upon truth. He has made his delight in doing what men say, and what the gods wish. He has given food to the hungry; drink to the thirsty; and clothes to the naked. His lips are pure, and his hands are pure. His heart weighs right in the balance. The departed fought on earth the battle of the good gods, as his Father, the Lord of the Invisible World, had commanded him. O God, the protector of him who has brought his cry unto thee, make it well with him in the world of Spirits!

*A portion of the Egyptian Book of the Dead, found in ancient tombs, written on papyrus,— 2000 B.C.*

May thy soul attain to the Creator of all mankind    These have found grace in the eyes of the Great God. They dwell in the abodes of glory, where the heavenly life is led.  The bodies which they have abandoned will repose forever in their tombs, while they will enjoy the presence of the Great God.

*Writing in Egyptian tombs,*— 2000 *B.C.*

---

The God of the Dead waits enthroned in immortal light to welcome the good into his kingdom of joy ; to the homes he had gone to prepare for them, where the One Being dwells beyond the stars.

*Oldest of the Vedas, Hindu,*— 1500 *B.C.*

---

Death does not differ at all from life.

*Thales, Grecian,*— *born* 640 *B.C.*

---

The evil-doer mourns in this world, and he will mourn in the next world : in both worlds has he sorrow.  He grieves, he is tormented, seeing the evil of his deeds.

The virtuous man rejoices in this world, and he will rejoice in another world : in both worlds hath he joy.  He rejoices, he exults, seeing the virtue of his deeds.

As kindred, friends, and dear ones salute him who hath travelled far and returned home safe, so will good deeds welcome him who goes from this world and enters another.

*Dhammapada, Buddha Sakya, Hindu,*— *born* 627 *B.C.*

The man who has constantly contended against evil, morally and physically, outwardly and inwardly, may fearlessly meet death; well assured that radiant Spirits will lead him across the luminous bridge into a paradise of eternal happiness.

Souls risen from the graves will know each other, and say, That is my father, or my brother, my wife, or my sister. The wicked will say to the good, Wherefore, when I was in the world, did you not teach me to act righteously? O ye pure ones, it is because you did not instruct me, that I am excluded from the assembly of the blest.

*Zendavesta, Persian, Zoroaster,—* 589 *B.C.*

---

When thou shalt have laid aside thy body, thou shalt rise, freed from mortality, and become a god of the kindly skies.

*Pythagoras, Grecian,— born* 580 *B.C.*

---

My body must descend to the place ordained, but my soul will not descend: being a thing immortal, it will ascend on high, where it will enter a heavenly abode.

*Heraclitus, Ephesian,—* 500 *B.C.*

---

The soul is the principle of life, which the Sovereign Wisdom employed to animate bodies. Matter is inert and perishable. The soul thinks, acts, and is immortal. . . . There is another invisible, eternal existence superior to this visible one, which does not perish when all things perish. Those who attain to this never return.

*Bhagavadgita, Hindu,—* 200 *B.C.*

The soul is not born; it does not die. It was not produced from any one, nor was any produced from it. Unborn, eternal, it is not slain, though the body is slain. Subtler than what is subtle, greater than what is great,— sitting, it goes far; sleeping, it goes everywhere. Thinking of the soul as unbodily among bodies, and firm among fleeting things, the wise man casts off all grief.

*Buddhist Scripture.*

The effect òf water poured on the root of a tree is seen aloft in the branches and fruit; so in the next world are seen the effects of good deeds performed here.

*Buddhist Scriptures, Siam.*

There are treasures laid up in the heart,— treasures of charity, piety, temperance, and soberness. These treasures a man takes with him beyond death, when he leaves this world.

*Buddhist Scriptures, Ceylon.*

Man never dies. The soul inhabits the body for a time, and leaves it again. The soul is myself: the body is only my dwelling-place. Birth is not birth: there is a soul already existent when the body comes to it. Death is not death: the soul merely departs, and the body falls. It is because men see only their bodies that they love life and hate death.

*Buddhist Scriptures, Chinese.*

The soul, which cannot die, merits all the moral and intellectual improvement we can possibly give it.  A Spirit, formed to live forever, should be making continual advances in virtue and wisdom. At death, such a soul is conducted by its invisible guardian to the heights of heavenly felicity, where it becomes the associate of the wise and good of all ages.

Is it not strange, my friends, that after all I have said to convince you I am going to the society of the happy, you still think this body to be Socrates ?  Bury my lifeless body where you please ; but do not mourn over it, as if *that* were Socrates. . . .

It would be wrong for me not to be grieved to die, if I did not think I should go to wise and good deities, and dwell with men who have departed from this life, and are better than any who are here.  That I shall go to deities who are perfectly good, I can assert positively, if I can assert any thing of the kind.  And be assured I hope to go and dwell among good men, though I would not positively assert that.  I entertain a good hope that something awaits those who die, and that it will be better for the good than for the evil, as has been said long since.

*Socrates, Grecian,*—469 *B.C.*

It is impossible there should be much happiness in this life; but there is great hope that after death every person may obtain what he most wishes for.  This doctrine is not new, but has been known both to Greeks and other nations. . . .

The soul of each of us is an immortal Spirit, and goes to other immortals to give an account of its actions. . . .

Can the soul be destroyed? No. But if in this present life it has shunned being governed by the body, and has governed itself within itself, and has separated from the body in a pure state, taking nothing sensual away with it, does it not then depart to that which resembles itself,—to the invisible, the divine, the wise, the immortal? And, on its arrival there, is it not freed from errors, ignorance, fears, wild passions, and all other human evils? Does it not in truth pass the rest of its existence with the gods? . . .

Those who have lived a holy life, when they are freed from this earth and set at large, will arrive at a pure abode above, and live through all future time. They will arrive at habitations more beautiful than it is easy to describe.

*Plato, Grecian,—* 429 *B.C.*

---

O glorious day, when I shall remove from this confused crowd to join the divine assembly of souls! For I shall go not only to meet great men, but also my own son. His spirit, looking back upon me, departed to that place whither he knew that I should soon come ; and he has never deserted me. If I have borne his loss with courage, it is because I consoled myself with the thought that our separation would not be for long.

*Cato (as quoted by Cicero), Roman,— born* 243 *B.C.*

When I consider the faculties with which the human soul is endowed,—its amazing celerity, its wonderful power of recollecting past events, and its sagacity in discerning the future, together with its numberless discoveries in the arts and sciences, —I feel a conscious conviction that this active, comprehensive principle cannot possibly be of a mortal nature.  And as this unceasing activity of the soul derives its energy from its own intrinsic and essential powers, without receiving it from any foreign or external impulse, it necessarily follows that its activity must continue forever.  I am induced to embrace this opinion, not only as agreeable to the best deductions of reason, but also in deference to the authority of the noblest and most distinguished philosophers.  I consider this world as a place which Nature never intended for my permanent abode;  and I look on my departure from it, not as being driven from my habitation, but simply as leaving an inn.

*Cicero, Roman,—born* 106 *B.C.*

————

In my Father's house are many mansions.  I go to prepare a place for you. . . .

They who shall be accounted worthy to obtain that world cannot die any more; for they are equal unto the angels.

Now that the dead are raised, even Moses showeth at the bush, when he called the Lord the God of Abraham, and the God of Isaac, and the God of Jacob ; for he is not a God of the dead but of the living.

*Jesus Christ, Israelite.  New Testament.*

Not by lamentations and mournful chants ought we to celebrate the funeral of a good man, but by hymns ; for, in ceasing to be numbered with mortals, he enters upon the heritage of a diviner life.

*Plutarch, Grecian,*— 50 *A.D.*

Is it a misfortune to pass from infancy to youth? Still less can it be a misfortune to go from this miserable life to that true life into which we are introduced by death. Our first changes are connected with the progressive development of life. The new change which death effects is only the passage to a more desirable perfection. To complain of the necessity of dying is to accuse Nature of not having condemned us to perpetual infancy.

*Gregory of Nyssa, early Christian Father,*— 394 *A.D.*

What if earth
Be but the shadow of heaven ? and things therein
Each to the other like, more than on earth is thought ?

*John Milton, English,*— 1667 *A.D.*

In Nature, everything is connected, like body and spirit. Our future destination is a new link in the chain of our being, which connects itself with the present link most minutely, and by the most subtle progression ; as our earth is connected with the sun, and as the moon is connected with our earth. When death bursts the bonds of limitation, God will transplant us, like flowers, into quite other fields, and surround us with entirely different circumstances. Who has not experienced what new faculties are given to the soul by a new situation,—faculties which, in our old corner, in the stifling atmosphere of old circumstances and occupations, we had never imagined ourselves capable of?   In these matters, we can do nothing but conjecture.   But wherever I may be, through whatever worlds I may be led, I know that I shall forever remain in the hands of the Father who brought me hither, and who calls me further on.

*Herder, German,*— 1774 *A.D.*

I trouble not myself about the manner of future existence.   I content myself with believing, even to positive conviction, that the Power which gave me existence is able to continue it in any form and manner he pleases, either with or without this body ; and it appears more probable to me that I shall continue to exist hereafter, than that I should have existence as I now have, before that existence began.

*Thomas Paine, American,*— 1795 *A.D.*

Life is a state of embryo, a preparation for life. A man is not completely born until he has passed through death.

*B. Franklin, American,*— 1776 *A.D.*

When we die, we shall find we have not lost our dreams : we have only lost our sleep.

*J. P. Richter, German,*— 1774 *A.D.*

Of what import this vacant sky, these puffing elements, these insignificant lives, full of selfish loves, and quarrels, and ennui? Every thing is prospective, and man is to live hereafter. That the world is for his education is the only sane solution of the enigma. All the comfort I have found teaches me to confide that I shall not have less in times and places that I do not yet know. I have known admirable persons, without feeling that they exhaust the possibilities of virtue and talent. I have seen glories of climate, of summer mornings and evenings, of midnight sky; I have enjoyed the benefits of all this complex machinery of arts and civilization, and its results of comfort. The Good Power can easily provide me millions more as good. All I have seen teaches me to trust the Creator for all I have not seen. Whatever it be which the great Providence prepares for us, it must be something large and generous, and in the great style of his works.

*R. W. Emerson, American,—* 19*th cent. A.D.*

---

We sometimes congratulate ourselves at the moment of waking from a troubled dream : it may be so after death.

*N. Hawthorne, American,—* 19*th cent. A.D.*

---

God is our Father. Heaven is his high throne, and this earth is his footstool. While we sit around, and meditate or pray, one by one, as we fall asleep he lifts us into his bosom, and our waking is inside the gates of an everlasting world.

*William Mountford, American,—* 19*th cent. A.D.*

We go to the grave of a friend, saying, A man
is dead; but angels throng about him, saying, A
man is born.

*H. W. Beecher, American,—* 19*th cent. A.D.*

———

This world is simply the threshold of our vast
life; the first stepping-stone from nonentity into
the boundless expanse of possibility. It is the
infant-school of the soul. The physical universe
spread out before us, and the spiritual trials and
mysteries of our discipline are simply our primer,
our grammar, our spelling dictionary, to teach us
something of the language we are to use in our
maturity.

*Starr King, American,—* 19*th cent. A.D.*

# Burial Service.

---

*FROM A. U. A. SERVICE BOOK.*

I AM the resurrection and the life, saith the Lord Jesus Christ : he that believeth in me, though he were dead, yet shall he live ; and whosoever liveth and believeth in me shall never die.

We brought nothing into this world, and it is certain that we can carry nothing out. The Lord gave, and the Lord hath taken away ; blessed be the name of the Lord.

All flesh is as grass, and all the glory of man as the flower of grass. The grass withereth, the flower fadeth ; but the word of our God endureth forever.

Let not your heart be troubled : ye believe in God, believe also in me. In my Father's house are many mansions : if it were not so, I would have told you. I go to prepare a place for you. And if I go and prepare a place for you, I will come again and receive you unto myself ; that where I am, there ye may be also.

Now is Christ risen from the dead, and become the first fruits of them that slept. For since by man came death, by man came also the resurrection of the dead. For as in Adam all die, even so in Christ shall all be made alive.

There is one glory of the sun, and another glory of the moon, and another glory of the stars · for one star differeth from another star in glory. So also is the resurrection of the dead. It is sown in corruption, it is raised in incorruption ; it is sown in dishonor, it is raised in glory ; it is sown in weakness, it is raised in power ; it is sown a natural body, it is raised a spiritual body.

As is the earthy, such are they also that are earthy ; and as is the heavenly, such are they also that are heavenly. And as we have borne the image of the earthy, we shall also bear the image of the heavenly.

Now this I say, brethren, that flesh and blood cannot inherit the kingdom of God ; neither can corruption inherit incorruption. For this corruptible must put on incorruption, and this mortal must put on immortality.

So when this corruptible shall have put on incorruption, and this mortal shall have put on immortality, then shall be brought to pass the saying that is written, Death is swallowed up in victory.

O death ! where is thy sting ? O grave ! where is thy victory ? The sting of death is sin, and the strength of sin is the law ; but thanks be to God, who giveth us the victory, through our Lord Jesus Christ.

Therefore, my beloved brethren, be ye steadfast, unmovable, always abounding in the work of the Lord, forasmuch as ye know that your labor is not in vain in the Lord.

I reckon that the sufferings of the present time are not worthy to be compared with the glory which shall be revealed to us. For eye hath not seen, nor ear heard, nor the heart of man conceived, the things which God hath prepared for them that love him.

Our light affliction, which is but for a moment, worketh for us a far more exceeding and eternal weight of glory ; while we look not at the things which are seen, but at the things which are not seen : for the things which are seen are temporal, but the things which are not seen are eternal. For we know that, if our earthly house of this tabernacle were dissolved, we have a building of God, a house not made with hands, eternal in the heavens.

Whom the Lord loveth, he chasteneth. If ye endure chastening, God dealeth with you as with sons. Now no chastening for the present seemeth to be joyous, but grievous ; nevertheless, afterward it yieldeth the peaceable fruit of righteousness unto them that are exercised thereby.

The trying of your faith worketh patience. Submit yourselves to God, and the Lord will raise you up.

Blessed be the God and Father of our Lord Jesus Christ, who, according to his abundant mercy, hath begotten us again to a lively hope, by the resurrection of Jesus Christ from the dead ; to an inheritance incorruptible and undefiled, and that fadeth not away, reserved in heaven for you.

We know in part, and we prophesy in part ; but when that which is perfect shall come, then that which is in part shall be done away. Now we see through a glass, darkly ; but then, face to face :

now I know in part; but then shall I know even as also I am known.

And I heard a great voice out of heaven, saying, Behold! the tabernacle of God is with men; and he will dwell with them, and they shall be his people, and God himself shall be with them, and be their God.

I heard a voice from heaven, saying unto me, Write, From henceforth blessed are the dead who die in the Lord. Even so, saith the Spirit; for they rest from their labors, and their works do follow them.

They shall hunger no more, neither thirst any more; neither shall the sun light on them, nor any heat. For the Lamb which is in the midst of the throne shall feed them, and shall lead them unto living fountains of waters; and God shall wipe away all tears from their eyes.

And there shall be no more death, neither sorrow, nor crying, nor pain: for the former things are passed away.

Behold, I come quickly; and my reward is with me, to give every man according as his work shall be. Blessed are they that do his commandments, that they may have right to the tree of life, and may enter in through the gates into the city.

Jesus said, Suffer the little children to come unto me, and forbid them not; for of such is the kingdom of God.

*Prayer may here be offered by the Minister, or said as follows:*

Holy Father, be thou blessed both now and

evermore ; for all that thou doest is good. Thou hast seen fit to take away one who is very dear to us. Give us, we beseech thee, the spirit of filial submission. Enable us to say, It is well, for the Lord hath done it. May we feel that thy will is better than any thing we can desire for ourselves, and may we find comfort in holy and happy thoughts of the unseen world. Bring home to our hearts the promises of thy Son to those who fall asleep in him.

O Lord, teach us how to live so as to please thee. May nothing cause us to forget that we are pilgrims and sojourners here, as all our fathers were ; and may we set our chief affections on those things which are above. Merciful Father, forgive us our sins, and raise us from the death of sin to the life of righteousness.

O Lord God, fill our hearts with gratitude for thy great loving kindness to us. When thou takest away, we see how much thou hast given. We thank thee for the sweet memory of blessings which are for a season withdrawn from us, and for the many blessings which yet remain, and for hopes which no earthly troubles can overshadow.

Blessed be thy name, O Lord, for the assurance of eternal life ; for the faith that, when the night of the grave is past, a glorious morning will come, when thou shalt wipe away all tears from our eyes, and there shall be no more death, neither sorrow, nor crying, nor pain. Let this immortal hope sustain us in our bereavement. May we embrace thy promises, and be thankful ; may we know that thou art God, and be still.

O Lord, most high, with thy whole Church throughout the world we give thee thanks for all thy faithful servants who, having witnessed a good confession, have left the light of their example to shine before thy people on earth. Blessed be the memory of all thy saints in our hearts.   Teach us, who now dwell upon earth, to practise their doctrine, to imitate their lives, and to follow their example as they have followed Christ and thee.

Hear, accept, and answer these our prayers, which we would offer to thee in the faith and spirit of thy Son.   Amen.

*A Hymn may here be sung.*

May the peace of God, which passeth understanding, and the comfort of the Holy Spirit, be in your hearts always.   Amen.

# Service at the Grave.

MAN that is born of woman is of few days, and full of trouble. He cometh forth like a flower, and is cut down; he fleeth also as a shadow, and continueth not.

In the midst of life, we are in death. Of whom may we seek for succor, but of thee, O Lord, in whom our souls do rest and hope?

We must work the work of Him that sent us while it is day; the night cometh, in which no man can work.

There the wicked cease from troubling, and the weary are at rest.

From henceforth blessed are the dead, who die in the Lord; even so saith the Spirit; for they rest from their labors, and their works do follow them.

*A Hymn may be sung here, or at the close of the service.*

Forasmuch as it hath pleased Almighty God to take unto himself the soul of his child, we therefore commit the body to the ground, earth to earth, ashes to ashes, dust to dust, in the living hope that, as he has borne the image of the earthy, so also he shall bear the image of the heavenly.

Let us pray:

Almighty God, with whom do live the spirits of them that depart hence in the Lord, and with whom the souls of the faithful are in joy and felicity : we thank thee for having given to us the dear friend whom thou hast now taken away, and for the blessed assurance of reunion in a better world. Oh, grant that we, with all who are departed in faith, may have our perfect consummation and bliss in thine eternal glory. Amen.

*The Lord's Prayer may here be said.*

The grace of our Lord Jesus Christ, and the love of God, and the fellowship of the Holy Spirit be with us all evermore. Amen.

# Poems.

---

NOTE.—Words or phrases may be changed or omitted to adapt the poem to the occasion.

---

## From " In Memoriam."

O, YET we trust that somehow good
    Will be the final goal of ill,
    To pangs of nature, sins of will,
Defects of doubt, and taints of blood;

That nothing walks with aimless feet;
    That not one life shall be destroyed,
    Or cast as rubbish to the void,
When God hath made the pile complete;

That not a worm is cloven in vain;
    That not a moth with vain desire
    Is shrivelled in a fruitless fire,
Or but subserves another's gain.

Behold, we know not any thing;
    I can but trust that good shall fall
    At last — far off — at last, to all,
And every winter change to spring.

So runs my dream: but what am I?
    An infant crying in the night;
    An infant crying for the light;
And with no language but a cry.

I falter where I firmly trod,
    And, falling with my weight of cares
    Upon the world's great altar-stairs
That slope through darkness up to God,

I stretch lame hands of faith, and grope
    And gather dust and chaff, and call
    To what I feel is Lord of all,
And faintly trust the larger hope.

This truth came, borne with bier and pall,
    I felt it when I sorrowed most,
    ' Tis better to have loved and lost,
Than never to have loved at all.

*Tennyson.*

------

## To J. S.

GOD gives us love.  Something to love
    He lends us; but, when love is grown
To ripeness, that on which it throve
    Falls off, and love is left alone.

This is the curse of time.  Alas!
    In grief I am not all unlearned;
Once through mine own doors Death did pass;
    One went, who never hath returned.

He will not smile — not speak to me
    Once more.  Two years his chair is seen
Empty before us.  That was he
    Without whose life I had not been.

Your loss is rarer; for this star
    Rose with you through a little arc
Of heaven, nor having wandered far
    Shot on the sudden into dark.

I knew your brother: his mute dust
    I honor, and his living worth:
A man more pure and bold and just
    Was never born into the earth.

I have not looked upon you nigh,
    Since that dear soul hath fallen asleep.
Great Nature is more wise than I:
    I will not tell you not to weep.

And though my own eyes fill with dew,
    Drawn from the spirit through the brain,
I will not even preach to you,
    " Weep, weeping dulls the inward pain."

Let Grief be her own mistress still:
    She loveth her own anguish deep
More than much pleasure. Let her will
    Be done—to weep or not to weep.

I will not say, "God's ordinance
    Of death is blown in every wind;"
For that is not a common chance
    That takes away a noble mind.

His memory long will live alone
    In all our hearts, as mournful light
That broods above the fallen sun,
    And dwells in heaven half the night.

Vain solace! Memory, standing near,
    Cast down her eyes, and in her throat
Her voice seemed distant, and a tear
    Dropt on the letters as I wrote.

I wrote I know not what. In truth
    How *should* I soothe you anyway,
Who miss the brother of your youth?
    Yet something I did wish to say.

For he too was a friend to me:
    Both are my friends, and my true breast
Bleedeth for both; yet it may be
    That only silence suiteth best.

Words weaker than your grief would make
    Grief more. 'Twere better I should cease,
Although myself could almost take
    The place of him that sleeps in peace.

Sleep sweetly, tender heart, in peace:
    Sleep, holy spirit, blessed soul,
While the stars burn, the moons increase,
    And the great ages onward roll.

Sleep till the end, true soul and sweet.
    Nothing comes to thee new or strange.
Sleep full of rest from head to feet;
    Lie still, dry dust, secure of change.

*Tennyson.*

## The Secret of Death.

"She is dead," they said to him. "Come away:
Kiss her and leave her, thy love is clay."

They smoothed her tresses of dark brown hair;
On her forehead of stone they laid it fair;

With a tender touch they closed up well
The sweet, thin lips that had secrets to tell;

And over her bosom they crossed her hands,
"Come away," they said, "God understands."

But he who loved her too well to dread
The sweet, the stately, the beautiful dead,

He lit his lamp, and took the key,
And turned it. Alone again,— he and she.

Then he said, "Cold lips and breast without breath,
Is there no voice, no language of death?

"See now, I listen with soul, not ear:
What was the secret of dying, dear?

"O perfect dead! O dead most dear!
I hold the breath of my soul to hear.

"There must be pleasure in dying, sweet,
To make you so placid from head to feet!

"I would tell you, darling, if I were dead,
And 'twere your hot tears upon my brow shed.

"You should not ask vainly with streaming eyes,
Which of all death's was the chief surprise?"

Who will believe what he heard her say,
With a sweet soft voice, in the dear old way?

"The utmost wonder is this : *I hear,*
*And see you, and love you, and kiss you, dear ;*

*"And am your angel, who was your bride,*
*And know that, though dead, I have never died."*

*Edwin Arnold.*

## Here and There.

HERE is the sorrow, the sighing,
  Here are the cloud and the night;
Here is the sickness, the dying,—
  There are the life and the light.

Here is the fading, the wasting,
  The foe that so watchfully waits;
There are the hills everlasting,
  The city with beautiful gates.

Here are the locks growing hoary,
  The glass with the vanishing sands;
There are the crown and the glory,
  The house that is made not with hands.

Here is the longing, the vision,
  The hopes that so swiftly remove;
There is the blessed fruition,
  The feast, and the fulness of love.

Here are the heart-strings a-tremble,
  And here is the chastening rod;
There is the song and the cymbal,
  And there is our Father and God.

*Alice Cary.*

------

## The Eternal Goodness.

WITHIN the maddening maze of things,
  And tossed by storm and flood,
To one fixed stake my spirit clings :
  I know that God is good.

I long for household voices gone,
  For vanished smiles I long;
But God hath led my dear ones on,
  And he can do no wrong.

I know not what the future hath
  Of marvel or surprise,
Assured alone that life and death
  His mercy underlies.

And if my heart and flesh are weak
  To bear an untried pain,
The bruised reed he will not break,
  But strengthen and sustain.

And so, beside the silent sea
  I wait the muffled oar;
No harm from him can come to me
  On ocean or on shore.

I know not where his islands lift
  Their fronded palms in air ·
I only know I cannot drift
  Beyond his love and care.

*Whittier.*

------

### From " Snow=Bound."

THE dear home faces whereupon
The fitful firelight paled and shone,
Henceforward, listen as we will,
The voices of that hearth are still;
Look where we may, the wide earth o'er,
Those lighted faces smile no more.
We tread the paths their feet have worn,
  We sit beneath their orchard trees,
  We hear, like them, the hum of bees,
And rustle of the bladed corn;
We turn the pages that they read,
  Their written words we linger o'er,
But in the sun they cast no shade,
No voice is heard, no sign is made,
  No step is on the conscious floor!
Yet love will dream, and faith will trust
(Since He who knows our need is just),
That somehow, somewhere, meet we must.

Alas for him who never sees
The stars shine through his cypress-trees!
Who, hopeless, lays his dead away,
Nor looks to see the breaking day
Across the mournful marbles play!
Who hath not learned, in hours of faith,
  The truth, to flesh and sense unknown,
That Life is ever Lord of Death,
  And Love can never lose its own.

*Whittier.*

## A Chant.

WHO is the angel that cometh?
  Life!
Let us not question what he brings,
  Peace or strife;
Under the shade of his mighty wings,
  One by one,
 Are his secrets told;
  One by one,
Lit by the rays of each morning sun,
 Shall a new flower its petals unfold,
 With the mystery hid in its heart of gold.
We will arise and go forth to greet him,
 Singing gladly, with one accord;
"Blessed is he that cometh
In the name of the Lord!"

Who is the angel that cometh?
  Pain!
Let us arise and go forth to greet him;
  Not in vain
Is the summons come for us to meet him;
  He will stay
And darken our sun;
  He will stay
A desolate night, a weary day.
 Since in that shadow our work is done,
 And in that shadow our crowns are won,
Let us say still, while his bitter chalice
 Slowly into our hearts is poured,—
"Blessed is he that cometh
In the name of the Lord!"

Who is the angel that cometh?
  Death!
But do not shudder, and do not fear;
  Hold your breath,
For a kingly presence is drawing near,
  Cold and bright
 Is his flashing steel,
  Cold and bright
The smile that comes like a starry light
 To calm the terror and grief we feel;
 He comes to help, and to save, and to heal.

Then let us, baring our hearts and kneeling,
　　Sing, while we wait this angel's sword,—
"Blessed is he that cometh
　　In the name of the Lord!"

*Adelaide A. Procter.*

## The Good Old Grandmother.

O, SOFTLY waves the silver hair
　　From off that aged brow!
That crown of glory, worn so long,
　　A fitting crown is now.

Fold reverently the weary hands
　　That toiled so long and well;
And, while your tears of sorrow fall,
　　Let sweet thanksgivings swell.

That life-work, stretching o'er long years,
　　A varied web has been;
With silver strands by sorrow wrought,
　　And sunny gleams between.

These silver hairs stole slowly on,
　　Like flakes of falling snow,
That wrap the green earth lovingly
　　When autumn breezes blow.

Each silver hair, each wrinkle there,
　　Records some good deed done;
Some flower she cast along the way,
　　Some spark from love's bright sun.

How bright she always made her home!
　　It seemed as if the floor
Was always flecked with spots of sun,
　　And barred with brightness o'er.

The very falling of her step
　　Made music as she went;
A loving song was on her lip,
　　The song of full content.

And now, in later years, her word
　　Has been a blessed thing
In many a home, where glad she saw
　　Her children's children spring.

Her widowed life has happy been
　With brightness born of heaven;
So pearl and gold in drapery fold
　The sunset couch at even.

O, gently fold the weary hands
　That toiled so long and well;
The spirit rose to angel bands,
　When off earth's mantle fell.

She's safe within her Father's house,
　Where many mansions be;
O, pray that thus such rest may come,
　Dear heart, to thee and me!

*Anonymous.*

---

### The Old Man's Funeral.

I SAW an aged man upon his bier;
　His hair was thin and white, and on his brow
A record of the cares of many a year,—
　Cares that were ended and forgotten now.
And there was sadness round, and faces bowed,
And woman's tears fell fast, and children wailed aloud.

Then rose another hoary man, and said,
　In faltering accents to that weeping train:
"Why mourn ye that our aged friend is dead?
　Ye are not sad to see the gathered grain,
Nor when their mellow fruit the orchards cast,
Nor when the yellow woods let fall the ripened mast.

"Ye sigh not when the sun, his course fulfilled,
　His glorious course, rejoicing earth and sky,—
In the soft evening, when the winds are stilled,
　Sinks where his islands of refreshment lie,
And leaves the smile of his departure spread
O'er the warm-colored heaven and ruddy mountain-head.

"Why weep ye then for him, who, having won
　The bound of man's appointed years, at last,
Life's blessings all enjoyed, life's labors done,
　Serenely to his final rest has passed;
While the soft memory of his virtues yet
Lingers, like twilight hues when the bright sun is set?

"His youth was innocent; his riper age
   Marked with some act of goodness every day;
And, watched by eyes that loved him, calm and sage,
   Faded his late declining years away:
Meekly he gave his being up, and went
To share the holy rest that waits a life well spent.

"That life was happy : every day he gave
   Thanks for the fair existence that was his;
For a sick fancy made him not her slave,
   To mock him with her phantom miseries;
No chronic tortures racked his aged limb,
For luxury and sloth had nourished none for him.

"And I am glad that he has lived thus long,
   And glad that he has gone to his reward;
Nor can I deem that nature did him wrong,
   Softly to disengage the vital cord;
For, when his hand grew palsied, and his eye
Dark with the mists of age, it was his time to die."

*Bryant.*

---

## From " Thanatopsis."

So LIVE, that when thy summons comes to join
The innumerable caravan which moves
To that mysterious realm where each shall take
His chamber in the silent halls of death,
Thou go not like the quarry-slave at night,
Scourged to his dungeon; but, sustained and soothed
By an unfaltering trust, approach thy grave
Like one who wraps the drapery of his couch
About him, and lies down to pleasant dreams.

*Bryant.*

---

## The Covered Bridge.

TELL the fainting soul in the weary form,
   There's a world of the purest bliss,
That is linked as that soul and form are linked
   By a covered bridge with this.

Yet to reach that realm on the other shore,
   We must pass through a transient gloom;
And must walk unseen, unhelped, and alone,
   Through that covered bridge,— the tomb.

But we all pass over on equal terms;
   For the universal toll
Is the outer garb, which the hand of God
   Has flung around the soul.

Though the eye is dim, and the bridge is dark,
   And the river it spans is wide,
Yet faith points through to a shining mount
   That looms on the other side.

To enable our feet in the next day's march
   To climb up that golden ridge,
We must all lie down for a one night's rest
   Inside of the *covered bridge.*

                    *David Barker.*

------

## The Reaper and the Flowers.

THERE is a Reaper, whose name is Death,
   And, with his sickle keen,
He reaps the bearded grain at a breath,
   And the flowers that grow between.

"Shall I have naught that is fair?" saith he;
   "Have naught but the bearded grain?
Though the breath of these flowers is sweet to me,
   I will give them all back again."

He gazed at the flowers with tearful eyes,
   He kissed their drooping leaves;
It was for the Lord of Paradise
   He bound them in his sheaves.

"My Lord has need of these flowerets gay,"
   The Reaper said, and smiled;
"Dear tokens of the earth are they,
   Where he was once a child.

"They shall all bloom in fields of light,
   Transplanted by my care,
And saints, upon their garments white,
   These sacred blossoms wear."

And the mother gave, in tears and pain,
   The flowers she most did love;
She knew she should find them all again
   In the fields of light above.

O, not in cruelty, not in wrath,
    The Reaper came that day;
'Twas an angel visited the green earth,
    And took the flowers away.

*Longfellow.*

---

## Resignation.

THERE is no flock, however watched and tended,
    But one dead lamb is there!
There is no fireside, howsoe'er defended,
    But has one vacant chair!

The air is full of farewells to the dying,
    And mournings for the dead;
The heart of Rachel, for her children crying,
    Will not be comforted!

Let us be patient!  These severe afflictions
    Not from the ground arise,
But oftentimes celestial benedictions
    Assume this dark disguise.

We see but dimly through the mists and vapors;
    Amid these earthly damps,
What seem to us but sad, funereal tapers
    May be heaven's distant lamps.

There is no Death!  What seems so is transition;
    This life of mortal breath
Is but a suburb of the life elysian,
    Whose portal we call Death.

She is not dead,— the child of our affection,
    But gone unto that school
Where she no longer needs our poor protection,
    And Christ himself doth rule.

In that great cloister's stillness and seclusion,
    By guardian angels led,
Safe from temptation, safe from sin's pollution,
    She lives, whom we call dead.

Day after day we think what she is doing
    In those bright realms of air;
Year after year, her tender steps pursuing,
    Behold her grown more fair.

Thus do we walk with her, and keep unbroken
    The bond which nature gives,
Thinking that our remembrance, though unspoken,
    May reach her where she lives.

Not as a child shall we again behold her;
    For, when with raptures wild
In our embraces we again enfold her,
    She will not be a child,

But a fair maiden, in her Father's mansion,
    Clothed with celestial grace;
And beautiful with all the soul's expansion
    Shall we behold her face.

And though at times, impetuous with emotion
    And anguish long suppressed,
The swelling heart heaves, moaning like the ocean
    That cannot be at rest,—

We will be patient, and assuage the feeling
    We may not wholly stay;
By silence sanctifying, not concealing,
    The grief that must have way.

                        *Longfellow.*

---

### Night and Death.

"MYSTERIOUS night! when our first parent knew
    Thee from report divine, and heard thy name,
    Did he not tremble for this lovely frame,
This glorious canopy of light and blue?
Yet, 'neath the curtain of translucent dew,
    Bathed in the rays of the great setting flame,
    Hesperus with the host of heaven came,
And lo! creation widened in man's view.
Who could have thought such darkness lay concealed
    Within thy beams, O sun! or who could find,
While leaf and fly and insect lay revealed,
    That to such countless orbs thou madest us blind!
Why do we, then, shun death with anxious strife?
If *light* can thus deceive, wherefore not *life?*"

                        *Blanco White.*

## The Two Mysteries.

[In the middle of the room, in its white coffin, lay the dead child, a nephew of
the poet. Near it, in a great chair, sat Walt Whitman, surrounded by little ones,
and holding a beautiful little girl in his lap. The child looked curiously at the
spectacle of death, and then inquiringly into the old man's face. "You don't
know what it is, do you, my dear?" said he. "We don't either."]

WE know not what it is, dear, this sleep so deep and still;
The folded hands, the awful calm, the cheek so pale and chill;
The lids that will not lift again, though we may call and call;
The strange, white solitude of peace that settles over all.

We know not what it means, dear, this desolate heart-pain,
This dread to take our daily way, and walk in it again.
We know not to what other sphere the loved who leave us go;
Nor why we're left to wonder still; nor why we do not know.

But this we know: our loved and dead, if they should come this
　　day,—
Should come and ask us, "What is life?" not one of us could say.
Life is a mystery as deep as ever death can be;
Yet, O, how sweet it is to us, this life we live and see!

Then might they say,—these vanished ones,—and blessed is the
　　thought!—
"So death is sweet to us, beloved, though we may tell you naught;
We may not tell it to the quick—this mystery of death,—
Ye may not tell us, if ye would, the mystery of breath."

The child who enters life comes not with knowledge or intent,
So those who enter death must go as little children sent.
Nothing is known. But I believe that God is overhead;
And as life is to the living, so death is to the dead.

*Unknown.*

————

## The Other Side.

CLIMBING the mountain's shaggy crest,
　　I wondered much what sight would greet
　　My eager gaze whene'er my feet
Upon the topmost height should rest.

The other side was all unknown;
　　But, as I slowly toiled along,
　　Sweeter to me than any song
My dream of visions to be shown.

At length the topmost height was gained;
  The other side was full in view;
  My dreams — not one of them was true,
But better far had I attained.

For far and wide on either hand
  There stretched a valley broad and fair,
  With greenness flashing everywhere,—
A pleasant, smiling, home-like land.

Who knows, I thought, but so 'twill prove
  Upon that mountain-top of death,
  Where we shall draw diviner breath,
And see the long-lost friends we love.

It may not be as we have dreamed,
  Not half so awful, strange, and grand;
  A quiet, peaceful, home-like land,
Better than e'er in vision gleamed.

*J. W. Chadwick*

---

## Auld Lang Syne.

It singeth low in every heart,
  We hear it each and all,—
A song of those who answer not,
  However we may call;
They throng the silence of the breast,
  We see them as of yore,—
The kind, the brave, the true, the sweet,
  Who walk with us no more.

'Tis hard to take the burden up,
  When these have laid it down;
They brightened all the joy of life,
  They softened every frown;
But, oh, 'tis good to think of them,
  When we are troubled sore!
Thanks be to God that such have been,
  Although they are no more!

More home-like seems the vast unknown,
  Since they have entered there;
To follow them were not so hard,
  Wherever they may fare;

They cannot be where God is not,
　　On any sea or shore ;
Whate'er betides, Thy love abides,
　　Our God, for evermore.

*J. W. Chadwick.*

---

## 𝕳𝖊 𝖜𝖍𝖔 𝕯𝖎𝖊𝖉 𝖆𝖙 𝕬𝖟𝖎𝖒.

HE who died at Azim sends
This to comfort all his friends:

Faithful friends ! It lies, I know,
Pale and white and cold as snow;
And ye say, "Abdallah's dead ! "
Weeping at the feet and head.
I can see your falling tears,
I can hear your sighs and prayers ;
Yet I smile and whisper this,—
" *I* am not the thing you kiss :
Cease your tears, and let it lie :
It *was* mine, it is not I."
Sweet friends ! what the women lave,
For the last sleep of the grave,
Is a hut which I am quitting,
Is a garment no more fitting,
Is a cage from which at last,
Like a bird, my soul hath passed.
Love the inmate, not the room,—
The wearer, not the garb,— the plume
Of the eagle, not the bars
That kept him from those splendid stars.

Loving friends ! be wise and dry
Straightway every weeping eye.
What ye lift upon the bier
Is not worth a single tear.
'Tis an empty sea-shell,— one
Out of which the pearl has gone.
The shell is broken, it lies there :
The pearl, the all, the soul, is here.
'Tis an earthen jar, whose lid
Allah sealed, the while it hid
That treasure of his treasury,
A mind that loved him ; let it lie !
Let the shard be earth's once more,

Since the gold is in his store!
Allah glorious! Allah good!
Now thy world is understood;
Now the long, long wonder ends;
Yet ye weep, my foolish friends,
While the man whom ye call dead,
In unspoken bliss, instead,
Lives and loves you,—lost, 'tis true,
For the light that shines for you;
But in the light ye cannot see
Of undisturbed felicity,—
In a perfect paradise,
And a life that never dies.
Farewell, friends! But not farewell:
Where I am, ye, too, shall dwell.
I am gone before your face
A moment's worth, a little space.
When ye come where I have stepped,
Ye will wonder why ye wept;
Ye will know, by true love taught,
That here is all, and there is naught.
Weep awhile, if ye are fain:
Sunshine still must follow rain;
Only not at death,— for death,
Now we know, is that first breath
Which our souls draw when we enter
Life, which is of all life centre.

Be ye certain all seems love,
Viewed from Allah's throne above;
Be ye stout of heart, and come
Bravely onward to your home!
La-il Allah! Allah la!
O love divine! O love alway!

He who died at Azim gave
This to those who made his grave.

*Edwin Arnold.*

------

## The Pescadero Pebbles.

WHERE slopes the beach to the setting sun,
  On the Pescadero shore,
Forever and ever the restless surf
  Rolls up with its sullen roar.

And grasping the pebbles in white hands,
  And chafing them together,
And grinding them against the cliffs
  In stormy and sunny weather,

It gives them never any rest:
  All day, all night, the pain
Of their long agony sobs on,
  Sinks, and then swells again.

And tourists come from every clime
  To search with eager care
For those whose rest has been the least;
  For such have grown most fair.

But yonder, round a point of rock,
  In a quiet, sheltered cove,
Where storm ne'er breaks and sea ne'er comes,
  The tourists never rove.

The pebbles lie 'neath the sunny sky
  In quiet evermore:
In dreams of everlasting peace,
  They sleep upon the shore.

But ugly and rough and jagged still
  Are they left by the passing years;
For they miss the beat of angry storms
  And the surf that drips in tears.

The hard turmoil of the pitiless sea
  Turns the pebble to beauteous gem.
They who escape the agony
  Miss also the diadem.

*M. J. S.*

---

### "He giveth His Beloved Sleep."

HE resteth now. No more his breast
  Heaves with its weary breath:
Pain sits no longer on the brow
  Where lies the calm of death.
Sunk to his rest, like tired child,
  He lies in slumber deep,
Soft folded in the arms of Him
  Who "giveth his belovéd sleep."

Nay, doth he rest? No: day nor night
  He resteth not from praise.
His spirit, winged with rapture, knows
  No more earth's weary ways;
But ever toward the Infinite
  His flight on, upward, doth he keep;
For he gives active tirelessness,
  Who "giveth his belovéd sleep."

And while we grope our doubtful way,
  Tear-blinded in the night,
He reads the meaning of our grief
  Clear writ in heavenly light.
And looking o'er the path he trod,
  Weary, oft-times, and rough and steep,
He knows 'twas goodness led him on,
  And gave to " his belovéd sleep."

We, heart-sore pilgrims, follow him:
  It is not for his fate we moan,
But that we " see his face no more,"
  And now must travel on alone.
He, standing on the hills of God,
  Doth brightly beckon while we weep.
We'll rest not here, but hasten on ·
The night is short, the morning's dawn
  Shall greet us rising from our sleep.

*M. J. S.*

## A. B. C.

WHEN falls the night upon the earth,
  And all in shadow lies,
The sun's not dead: his radiance still
  Beams bright on other skies.

And when the morning star fades out
  On the pale brow of dawn,
Though lost awhile to earthly eyes,
  It still keeps shining on.

Some other world is glad to see
  Our star that's gone away:
The light whose going makes our night
  Makes somewhere else a day.

The feet that cease their walking here,
  Grown weary of earth's road,
With tireless strength go travelling
  The pathway up to God.

The hands whose patient fingers now
  Have laid earth's labors by,
With loving skill have taken up
  Some higher ministry.

The eyes that give no longer back
  The tender look of love,
Now, with a deathless gleam, drink in
  God's beauteous world above.

The lips whose sweet tones made us ask
  If angels sweeter sung,
Though silent here, make heaven glad
  With their melodious tongue.

And, though her body lies asleep,
  Our favorite is not dead:
She rises from dark death's bright birth,
  " With joy upon her head."

And she is just our loved one still,
  And loves us now no less:
She goes away to come again,—
  To watch us, and to bless.

And though we cannot clasp her hand,
  Nor look upon her face,
Nor listen to her voice again,
  Nor watch her ways of grace,

Still we can keep her memory bright,
  And walk the way she trod,
And trust she waits until we come
  Up to the house of God.

Let us be thankful, through our tears,
  That she was ours so long,
And try to lift our tones of grief
  T' accord with her heaven song.

                                       *M. J. S.*

## G. M.

Oh, what is all that can be done,
　　And what is all that can be said?
When all is past, the fact remains
　　That *he*, my noble one, is dead.

Friends gather round and speak to me,
　　But can they make *him* speak once more?
I see them coming, but I hear
　　Not *his* loved footfall on the floor.

They clasp my hand in sympathy;
　　But, oh! *his* hand is still and cold:
They look upon me, but *his* eyes
　　Will look no more the love of old.

O friends, your sympathy is dear,
　　But who can give *him* back to me?
Empty and poor is all the world,
　　Since I *his* face no more can see.

I do not mourn a common loss.
　　O merchants, have you known of one,
A truer, cleaner-handed man
　　Than he whose earthly work is done?

Tell me, O friends, if anywhere,
　　In all your circles, far or near,
You've found a firmer, truer friend
　　Than this fast friend that sleepeth here?

O mothers, who with love and pride,
　　In all the years since time begun,
Have trained your children, tell me where
　　You've found a truer, tenderer son!

O husbands, wives, in all the earth,
　　Was any less disposed to roam?
One who was purer in his love,
　　Or more devoted to his home?

O country, in your hour of need,
　　When swords were crossed in bitter strife,
What nobler patriot did you find,
　　One truer to your perilled life?

If "trees are by their fruitage known,"
  O God, who see'st the "inner part,"
Then search him through, and Thou shalt find
  That he was sound and true at heart.

But what can this avail me now?
  Because in him there was no dross,
Because my memories are so fair,
  Therefore is mine the greater loss.

But — God forgive me! — though I bear
  A pain that words can never tell,
Yet somehow I must still believe
  That what so crushes me is well.

The memory of his noble life
  Shall still inspire me; and some day
The clouds may lift, and light once more
  Shine round about my darkened way.

I know *he*'d have me hopeful still:
  Let me look up, then, through my tears.
He'll not return; but I shall hope
  To find *him* in the happier years.

*M. J. S.*

---

### Kisagotami.

Founded on a beautiful Buddhist legend. Kisagotami is the mother's name.

WITH fixed white face the mother goes,
  With her dead child at her breast;
In the house where no one has ever died
  She will find relief and rest.
" Oh, tell me! where is the place
  That has ne'er seen a dead white face?"

From village to village, from town to town,
  She wanders the country o'er;
At her asking, ever the tears fall down,
  Death has passed through every door.
" Oh, tell me! is there *no* place
  That has ne'er seen a dead white face?"

"No place, no place, my child," said then
  A white-haired man, and old:
"The living are few, to the numbers vast,
  The earth in her arms doth hold."
"But is there *never* a place
  That has ne'er seen a dead white face?"

"Yes, child," the old man said at last:
  "There is one place we trust;
But only they find it who have passed
  Through the gateway of the dust."
"Sleep, then, my child: thy face
  Sees the land where death has no place."

*M. J. S.*

---

### The Finished Life.

THERE'S a beauty of the spring-time
  With its fresh grass and its flowers,
With the song-birds in the branches,
  And the children's happy hours

But there's no less of beauty
  When the leaves turn gold and brown
In the shortening days of autumn,
  When far south the birds have flown.

If the rough hand of the tempest
  Tear away the fresh young leaves,
Over youthful vigor wasted,
  Who can wonder if one grieves?

But when from autumn branches
  Drop the brown leaves one by one,
It seems as fair and fitting
  As the setting of the sun.

The old man by the fireside
  Looks back through tender tears,
And says, "With wife and children
  I trod long, happy years."

The old man by the window
  Looks o'er the city ways,
And says, "Success and honor
  Were mine in long gone days.

"I've seen the world's fair beauty;
  I've tasted all its sweet;
And now, past two and three score,
  My life is all complete.

"The face of her who loved me
  Now beckons far away:
I've wrought the work God gave me,
  Then wherefore should I stay?"

And who, O friends, would keep him?
  Sound no funereal knell;
Say of his life, "'*Twas blessed!*"
And of his death, "'*Tis well!*"

*M. J. S.*

---

## "Better Off."

"HE's better off." With words like these
  Kind friends their comfort try to speak.
None doubts it of a man like him;
  Yet far off sound the words, and weak.

The heart that loves is not content,
  However well the loved one be,
To have him happy far away,
  But cries, "I want him still *with me!*"

That other country may be fair,
  Brighter than aught the earth has shown,
But better any place with him,
  Than to be left here all alone.

Thus pleads the heart that God has made,—
  He cannot blame what he has given,—
For heaven without love could not be,
  And, having love, the earth is heaven.

The folded hands, the closing eyes,
  The yielding up of failing breath,—
These not the worst: to tear apart
  Two hearts that truly love *is death.*

Since love is all the joy of life,
  In earth below or heaven above,
Somewhere, we cannot help but trust,
  God keeps for us the ones we love.

Like ships the storms drive far apart
  Wide o'er the sea 'neath cloud and sun,
We'll still sail for the self-same port,
  And meet there when the voyage is done.

And as we tell the story o'er,
  How we were driven by the blast,
More sweet will be those sunny hours
  By contrast with the sorrows past.

M. J. S.

---

### Death's Lesson.

FROM these closed eyes, and these white lips
  Where loving smiles no longer play,
What, to the ear that silence hears,
  Does Death to us, the living, say?

"Sweet friends, the words of love you wish
  You'd said to me while I could hear
Take heed, in days to come, you speak
  To living ones who still are near.

"No more for me can you do aught,
  Save make the flowers bloom where I sleep;
But hearts of living ones still ache,
  And eyes of living ones still weep.

"Pour out on them the love and care
  You wish you could on me bestow;
Then, when some other falls asleep,
  O'er vain regrets no tears shall flow."

Death, then, would teach us how to live,
  How we shall die need give no care,—
Live as we'll wish we had; and then
  Death's face becomes divinely fair.

M. J. S.

---

### Child with the Snowy Cheek.

CHILD with the snowy cheek,
Child with the stainless brow,
  Thy white-robed form and look so meek
Are as an angel's now.

Death's mystery hath cast
Its strangeness o'er thy face,
　But the angel marred not as he passed
One line of its tender grace.

He but folded the waxen hands,
Sent sleep on the gladsome eyes,
　And wrapped thee round with the viewless bands
Of death's great, still surprise.

Now into the upper life,
Into realms of infinite peace,
　Thou hast entered at once, untouched by the strife
That comes with our life's increase.

Into the infinite love,
Into the cloudless light,
　Into the welcome that waited above,—
Below thee, the storm and night.

Saved from the toilsome way
We travel with weary feet,
　From the bitterness hid in the cup alway,
Whose first taste is so sweet.

The base and the unkind,
The cruel and the untrue,
　Soiling and stain of the deathless mind,
Fair child, are not for you.

For you there is gladness and rest
Where the white-robed singers stand,
　Where pain is forgotten and sorrow is blest,
In the soul's own fatherland.

Where the little ones of earth,
In gardens and meadows broad,
　Wandering and playing, make musical mirth
By the soft-flowing river of God.

But we! In a world of pain,
We linger and weep and wait;
　And we strive in vain any glimpse to gain
Of thee and the Beautiful Gate.

For the gate that is gold to thee,
Golden and jewelled and bright,
　Is wrapped in gloom on the side we see,—
Its sentinels, Fear and Night.

But the gate of gloom and of gold
Will open to us some day,
On hinges of silence backward rolled;
And Fear will vanish away.

And Night into Morning will change,
As the light of the Land comes out,
And a rapture, sudden and sweet and strange,
Succeed to our trouble and doubt.

Oh, blessed and strong and sweet
The hope of that coming time,
When thy welcoming hands our hands shall meet
In the gate of the Life Sublime;

In the gate of the City of God;
In the gate of the Infinite Peace;
In the sweet dawn-light that shall shine abroad
O'er the fields of our love's increase.

*W. H. Savage.*

---

## The Home-Seeker.

### I.

TWILIGHT falls: a tiny maiden
Cometh up the village street;
Vagrant locks, all dewy-laden,
Eager eyes, and tired feet
Hath the shadowy little maiden.

Tired of wandering and of playing,
Up the dim street, see her come;
Hurrying now, and now delaying,
Toward the rest and love of home,
Comes the maiden from her playing.

### II.

See again! a woman hasting
Down a shadowy, sunset way,
Loving, anxious glances casting
Through the twilight soft and gray;
Homeward, love-ward she is hasting.

Laughing children run to meet her
From the home-door, open wide;
Loving words and kisses greet her,
Pattering feet run by her side;
All the home comes forth to meet her.

### III.

Look once more! a pilgrim weary
Standeth in the twilight gray;
  All around is strange and dreary,
  And she asks, with plaintive query,
"Can you show the homeward way?
  Lead me homeward: I am weary."

Then a Presence stood to guide her,
Pointed where the way did lie;
  Gently spoke, and walked beside her
  To a gateway dim and high.
"Home," she breathed, with restful sigh,
  To the Presence that did guide her.

### IV.

Homeward still, the tiny maiden,
Motherhood, love and care laden,
Age, with weight of years oppressed,
Homeward turn for love and rest.
And the home, with open door,
Waits with "Welcome" evermore.

W. H. Savage.

---

## The Sunset Way.

THE sun that sinks when Eventide
Sits veiled, with dewy eyes,
  Beside the gateway of the West,
On other lands doth rise.

The life that sinks, when failing breath
Is hushed to stillness at the last,
  Veiled in the mystery of death,
Is as a star when clouds sweep past.

Night's gateway is the gate of Dawn,
Death's gate the gate of Birth;
  The sun that set is shining on;
The soul now lost to earth,—

  Emerging from the brief eclipse
By evening shadows cast,
  Smiles, star-like, in that other morn
Where pain and death are past.

And, spreading fair and sweet before,
　Are fields of rest and peace,
　　Where Joy doth sing for evermore,
　And love doth still increase.

　O friends, who take the sunset way
　And fear the coming night,
　　Each sunset is a birth of day,
　Your steps approach the light.

　Love cannot die: eternity
　Shall keep your sacred trust, be sure;
　　"For God is Love," and heaven must be
　A home where love may dwell secure.

　Look onward! High above the tomb
　The omens of the morning shine!
　　The evening has its transient gloom,
　The morrow comes with beams divine.

*W. H. Savage.*

---

## As God Will.

IF I were told that I must die to-morrow,
　　That the next sun
Which sinks should bear me past all fear and sorrow
　　For any one,
All the fight fought, and all the journey through,
　　What should I do?

I do not think that I should shrink or falter,
　　But just go on,
Doing my work, nor change, nor seek to alter,
　　Aught that is gone;
But rise and move and love and smile and pray
　　For one more day.

And, lying down at night for a last sleeping,
　　Say in that ear
Which hearkens ever, "Lord, within thy keeping,
　　How should I fear?
And when to-morrow brings Thee nearer still,
　　Do Thou thy will."

I might not sleep, for awe ; but peaceful, tender,
    My soul would lie
All the night long; and, when the morning splendor
    Flashed o'er the sky,
I think that I could smile, could calmly say;
    " It is his day."

But if a wondrous hand from the blue yonder
    Held out a scroll,
On which my life was writ, and I with wonder
    Beheld unroll
To a long century's end its mystic clew,
    What should I do?

What could I do, O blessed Guide and Master,
    Other than this,—
Still to go on as now, not slower, faster,
    Nor fear to miss
The road, although so very long it be,
    While led by Thee?

Step by step, feeling Thou art close beside me,
    Although unseen;
Through thorns, through flowers, whether tempest hide Thee
    Or heavens serene;
Assured thy faithfulness cannot betray,
    Nor love decay.

I may not know my God; no hand revealeth
    Thy counsels wise;
Along the path no deepening shadow stealeth ;
    No voice replies
To all my questioning thoughts, the time to tell:
    And it is well.

Let me keep on abiding and unfearing
    Thy will always,
Through a long century's ripe fruition
    Or a short day's.
Thou canst not come too soon ; and I can wait,
    If Thou come late.

                          *Anonymous.*

CPSIA information can be obtained
at www.ICGtesting.com
Printed in the USA
LVOW10s0348200717

541972LV00031B/1015/P